Upon Becoming a New Creature

By
Nicole Mangum

Published by Liberation's Publishing
PO Box 1038
West Point MS 39773

ISBN 978-0-9891348-1-1

This book is dedicated to my teacher Mr. Griffin. He taught me the importance of becoming a new creature.

Rebirth

A New Creature

John 3:7 "...Ye must be born again."

It is through much suffering
That you become a new creature in Christ
It is as if every part within you shall fail
And through much pain
You learn to praise the
Creator more abundantly
After the loosing of your sanity
You are given the true mind of Christ
And once your body is so ragged and torn
The Lord will wrap you in swaddling clothes
To bandage your wounds
And one day you will awaken
Shedding the sinful body
As if emerging from a cocoon
And like a butterfly you will have wings
And on this earth you shall see and feel
The Kingdom of Heaven

Upon Entering the Kingdom

Luke 12:32 "fear not little flock, for it is your Father's good pleasure to give you the Kingdom."

*My soul blossomed
From an empty shell piece by piece
The struggles and burdens of this world
Fell away like the dropping of a robe
I entered into the Kingdom
And the souls of old folk, Saints, and Angels
Came to share in my happiness
They rejoiced with me
I felt so welcomed as they said
"Hello Darling, we're so glad you made it."
What a wonderful place God's heaven,
Yes, what a wonderful glorious place*

The Spirit

John 3:5 "Except a man be born of water and of spirit he cannot enter into the Kingdom of God."

The spirit of the Lord is all around me
And I cannot keep still
The spirit of the Lord is deep inside me
And my whole soul is filled
Sometimes I want to shout
Sometimes want to cry
Sometimes I want to run,
I feel like I can fly
How could I turn away
From all the Love you gave me
How could I return to the life
From which you saved me
My feet are planted firm
And I shall not be moved
I will serve you Lord
until heaven and earth are moved

Glory

Isaiah 60:1 "ARISE shine for thy light is come,
And the glory of the Lord is risen upon thee."

I am like the wind, so soft, so light
My life has become an endless dream
In the midst of trouble I am safe
Weapons melt before me like a spring rain
I am peace, I am peace personified
I lounge in the eye of the storm
I am love, love overflowing unto the ground
Washing away hate with a quiet storm
Can you hear the peace?
Can you feel the love?
It is God
God with us

His Grace is Sufficient

John8:7 "...the words that I speak unto you
They are spirit and they are life."

From this broken down body
Life shoots forth like a tree
Planted by the river of Jordan
We are seeds
Seeds planted in the dirt and soil
Of this corrupt world
And it is the constant showering of rain
And the beating down of the Son
That allows us to live again
Not as before
but as new creatures
Spirit men and women
Connected directly to the love of God
By the union of his Holy Spirit to our souls
Be free, for the Son has given it to you
Your freedom in a bound world
New life, New creature, True creature,
Full of light

I Live

John 5:25 "...the dead shall hear the voice of the Son of God and they that hear shall live."

I awoke
Praising God in the most beautiful way
My movements full of grace,
my voice like an angel
I swayed like the wind
Bowed like the limbs of a willow
The coolness of the Lord surrounded me
We were one like leaves floating on the wind
What peace, what love,
love manifest as the wind
And covered me with peace
and filled my soul
I am transformed a new creature
Holy and acceptable
I walk in spirit and truth
I am light, a watchtower that cannot be hid
Only shine beautifully flow
Beautifully love beautifully

I Shall Give Me

2 Corinthians 6:16 "...for ye are the temple of the living God...I will dwell in them, and walk in them"

This beauty that you see
Is far deeper than it appears
For it has been shaped by
the washing away of sin
And as the river flows through
the Grand Canyon
My father has created
yet another master piece
That is me
Worthy to house the finer things
The Water of Life, the Holy Spirit of God
I know I shine bright like the Son
It is the righteousness of the
Saints that are shining down on me
What else could I build for the Lord?
When he fills the whole world
What royal tapestry of silk or wool
Could I use for his feet.
When all he desired was me

My Cup Overfloweth

Psalms 34:8 "O taste and see that the Lord is good"

I have tasted and seen
That the Lord is good
So I asked for a cup. I drank and drank
Until it seemed like something in me burst
It started at the pit of my soul
Flowing upward past my heart
It flowed up through my out stretched
Hands giving praise to God
It flowed from my mouth,
My ears and tongue
Everlasting life I know I've won
The living waters flow through me
And I am planted like a tree
By the river of Jordan

Peace

Ephesians 4:4 "There is one body and one spirit..."

Man cannot disturb my peace
It is as strong as steel yet soft as snow
What a wonderful combination
This peace and love of God
It is unexplainable in the words of man
It is the same peace that holds the heavens
Yet the same peace that inflames our sun
What a wonderful combination
This peace and love of God
I could stand in it all day and not be moved
Yet be everywhere
What a wonderful combination
This peace and love of God
No other power in the world
can stand against it.
It is in all things and the source of all things

Planted

Psalms 22:30 *"a seed shall serve him..."*

A seed
Such a small commonly thing
But once planted watered and fed
By the Son
Produces such a magnificent
And wonderful thing
Something uncorrupt and straightened
Smooth no longer ragged
Peace no more disorder
Love no more hate
Quiet within the storm

Grace

Ephesians 2:8 "for by grace are ye saved through faith, And not of yourselves, it is the gift of God"

No greater love than
Jesus laying down his life for my soul
I cannot comprehend
the hardship that it tolled,
He has always loved me
Forgiving again, again, and again
My disobedience and defiance.
My swerving right and left
Not once did he deny my entry back
onto his path
Not once did he turn me away.
My repentance not accept
Oh Jesus thank you for your mercy,
for Grace, your love
Because without either my victory
I would not have won

Take Hold of Me

Psalms 38:18 "For I will declare mine iniquity,
I will be sorry for my sin."

Lord what are you saying to me?
I'm lost in this storm.
It's dark and I can't see.
I'm so full of sin. I can't hear you.
I'm so wrapped up in myself.
I can't feel you.
I've got this cloud on my soul.
I'm cold. I'm not strong.
I need your arms. Take hold of me.

The Master's Rest

Matthews 11:28 "Come unto me, all ye that labor And are heavy laden,
And I will give you rest."

There is no love
More beautiful than yours
There is no power more lovely to behold
Within your arms I've found protection
Within your arms I'm safe from harm
Journey with me
Into my Master's Peace
Let us stand in his presence
And from life have relief

All This For Me

Psalms 37:4 "Delight thyself also in the Lord:
And he shall give thee the desires of your heart."

What is this glory
That has been showered down on me
It is the love of God.
His very essence.
The Father's love.
I am his child.
He carries me in his bosom.
I am safe.
For the first time in my life
I have no fear.
Every need is met before I speak.
I shall never leave this place.

Love

Love

Genesis 2:18 "God Said It is not good for the man to be alone."

*Whoever said love does not hurt
has never been in love
To live my life without you near
takes strength from God above
My heart longs for your kisses
My body longs for your touch
What God has put together
should never be apart
Our first father Adam
was not tricked or deceived
He just could not imagine
his life without Eve*

Anxious

Song of Solomon 5:2 "I sleep but my heart waketh..."

Your love
Takes me to heights of ecstasy
I am afloat
On a river that runs into paradise
I am a leaf
Caught up in an autumn breeze
Flowing upward then
Slowly ...
Slowly...
Slowly...
Falling back down to earth
Anxiously awaiting its next ascension

I Love You

*Song of Solomon 7:10 "I am my beloved's
And his desire is toward me."*

*I love you
Like the earth loves the rain
Your love is cool, Refreshing
Thirst quenching
And
Just like Earth
I could not survive
If your love stopped falling
I would just dry up and die
Becoming a barren desert*

Soft

Song of Solomon 2:6 "His left hand
is under my head And his right hand doth embrace me."

Your love is soft
Like a cool breeze on a warm day
Like the sound of a quiet storm at midnight
Through a cracked windowsill
Like water,
Flowing over a parched tongue
Like a mother's breast
To her lover and her young

My Lord

Ephesians 5:33 "...and the wife see that she reverence her husband."

My Lord leads me
My husband my head
I follow behind closely
He gladly allows me to walk beside him
But I choose the safety of behind him
Where I am free to watch his strength
As He forges ahead
Clearing our path
So I can walk without stumbling
I am his Queen
He is my King
He falls that I may stand

With you
I am King

Eph 5:28 ..."He that loveth his wife Loveth himself..."

When I look at you
I see a part of me that is perfect
Strong and Gentle
Though I have the fate of man
I elevate you as a queen, because
This world beats me down so profusely
It takes everything within me
You replenish me
Without you I am just a man.
With you I am a king
Worthy of the finest things
Your love makes me walk with pride
Stare evil right within the eye
Because within you my prize lies
My seed barer, my lover, my wife

This Love

Eph 5:23 "...for the husband is the head of the wife..."

What kind of love is this
The more I give
The more is taken
What kind of love is this
When it feels like my heart is aching
To stand against the wind
To speak unto the storm
To overcome the world
For the sake of a little girl
Who at the start of time
Was deceived by a lie
That was planted in her mind
But this love reversed time
So that everything you see
Would result in good for you and me
And death was over come
Before it was begun

She

Genesis 24:67 "...And she became his wife; And he loved her..."

When she smiles my world is brighter
When she is strong my strength is mightier
When she breathes I breathe lighter
I was lost and she became my guider
Is this what HE meant
When from heaven HE sent
Me this help meet
Whose lips are the richest sweet
I have ever tasted
Whose love is the strongest
I have ever faced
It humbles me to my knees
Do all I can to please she
That this grace may never leave me
For I was thirsty and she gave me
Straight from the hand of God Our Father
A taste of the living waters

This Is The Day

Psalms 118:24 "This is the day which the LORD hath made; We will rejoice and be glad in it."

This is the day that's so full of grace
There is joy in this day, Peace in this day
On this day
When two lonely hearts
have finally become a part of one
A life has just begun
This is the day
With the passage of time
and the opening of my eyes
I began to see
That you were a part of me
Part of my destiny
I never would have dreamed
That you were the king
Waiting to carry me into my destiny
So many times you'd smile and pass by
Well you were just planting seeds
Now The Fathers love has rained on me
Your love has become our tree
Rooted deep inside of HE
I am so ready to be your queen
You are my destiny

This is the day

"Happy 22nd Anniversary"

Ephesians 5:22 "Husbands love you wives..."

A woman was made from love to be loved.
It is the only way she will flourish and grow.
When you look at me you see a man that loves you.
A man that hurts when you hurt
and laughs when you laugh.
I need you. I love you.
I am your Adam.
You are the rib that was taken from me so long ago.
Now you are returned.
I was bruised and worn, but with you I was restored.
You are my Eve the mother of all living,
Everything I place in your hands multiplies.
You make my burden easier.
With you I will till the ground.
As you wipe the sweat from my brow.
We will create our piece of
The Kingdom of God.

Wonderful

Isaiah 9:6 "...and his name shall be called Wonderful..."

I held wonderful by the palm of its hand
It was tall handsome
With a smile like a three
year old at Christmas
It felt good to the touch
Made you feel safe
And kept you warm
Wonderful made you want to take each day
Like you were loving for the first time
It was so good you wanted it to last forever
And just when you thought it would fade
Wonderful makes things wonderful all over again

A
Word
From God

Vanity

Psalms 94:11 "The Lord knoweth the thoughts of man,
That they are vanity."

With all your titles and degrees,
If you have not love so you have nothing
I cannot understand
When God places within your hand
A child that is so innocent a blessing that is heaven sent
With arrogance you disregard
and write them off as county wards
Yet Sundays you shout "I believe"
While inside your soul disagrees
And with all your titles and degrees
You have not love so you have nothing
The titles you greatly aspire
And the praise and glory you desire
Mean nothing when your soul retires
Your body is laid down to rest
And before our Father you must attest
It shall all be in vain as our Father's voice proclaims
"I never knew you;
you see, my righteousness you did not seek
My children you have left for dead
But by my grace they still got feed
Get away from me unrighteous seed
you worker of iniquity
And from Hell you lift up your eyes
And no title there will compromise
Your position there within the fire

Great Teacher

Job 27:11"I will teach you by the hand of God..."

Thank God for a Great Teacher
You have a story to tell
That through great struggle and pain
Righteousness did prevail
One night when you retired,
A Miracle transpired
In your heart you understood
that there is no greater good
Than to give of yourself
and hope later one would accept
This wonderful gift you chose to give
So a better life they may live
Just like Christ on Christmas Day
Was born to show the way
And an anointing each year is born
On each glorious Christmas Morn
And I wish it well for you and
The ones you love great and few

We Are One Body

Philippians 2:2 "...that ye be like minded, having the same love being of one accord one mind..."

Come inside my family as you are
We are all the same, Children of God
O, I see the deception the devil would have me believe
But, God has given me my sight
It is you I see before me
Your soul is just like mine longing to be free
We are strangers here this is not our eternity
Please come inside my family,
There is plenty of space
The father has given us a double portion
Of his mercy and grace
We are the righteousness of God
Redeemed of the human race

Rejoice

Psalm 23:2 "...he maketh me to lie down
In green pastures..."

The harvest is in. It is time to live
The meadows are green. I shall run through them
With my arms raised in praise to the Lord
My soul has longed for this day
The Savior has returned. And with him his reward
Who cares about tears shed through the years?
They are being wiped away never to return
In the form of despair
Tears of joy will never cease to be
My father it was you. You were here all the time
Leading me, ordering me, rearranging me
Storm after storm, hurt after hurt, loss after loss
To stand in your glory, by your glory
Because of your Grace

My Children

2 Corinthians 6:18 "Ye shall be my sons
And daughters, saith the Lord Almighty."

Do you think I would leave you alone
In this world without my love
I love you.
Do you think I have forsaken you
I made you.
Do you think your cries fall upon deaf ears
I hear you.
I fill the whole entire world, and
My love is from everlasting to everlasting.
I have withheld nothing
For the sake of your souls
Before you were...I love you
Unto death...I love you
When you return ...I love you.

Life's Question

Job 7:1 "...is there not an appointed time
To man upon this earth?"

If heaven is the ultimate goal
Of a servant of God
Why is loosing someone you love
So painful and hard
Could it be that we in our selfishness
Want to keep them here
Never to reach their mansion
With streets paved of gold
To sip milk from honeycombs
It's hard not to see their face
It's hard to know they want be home
But, if you're quiet and at peace
You can still feel their souls

Thy Salvation Cometh

Exodus 16:12 "I have heard the murmurings
Of the children of Israel."

I looked upon you and cried,
"Why are my children suffering?"
Is there no balm in Gilead?
Is Israel a servant?
Is he a home born slave?
Then I saw that no one lead you to the balm
Nor bothered to fetch it for you
I saw how you were distressed
sheep without a shepherd
Unwashed, in need of salt
Behold your salvation cometh
With him is your reward
You shall be cleansed your beauty restored

Going Through

Genesis 42:36 "...All these things are against me."

Momma can you hear me
Can you feel me in your soul?
I'm trying hard to keep my head up
I'm trying hard not to let go
I know the bed you make
In it you must lay down
But all this pain and loss
Has got me level to the ground
Just don't stop praying me through
I know God spared me because of you
I will lift my head up to the hills
Try hard with faith to discipline my will
And to your love I will hang on
Until my Savior sends me home

Freedman

2 Corinthians 3:14 "...But their minds were blinded..."
January 1, 1863 I am the product of slavery.
And though I have been freed, Freedom eludes me.
You are my master. I am your slave.
This I know. Freedom ... I do not understand.
Three hundred years went into making me
And the stripes on my back bare witness of my initiation
Into this order of the slave
This order of the freedman ... I do not understand.
It is now January 1, 2006.
And I am still the product of slavery
I have been freed One hundred and forty three years
And Freedom still eludes me.
You are still my master. I am still your slave.
Though I live in a freedman's house
Receive a freedman's wage
The drugs in my veins and
the darkness of my soul
Define me as a bound man
I envied you and your freedom.
The harvests that you yielded
I longed to eat the fruit of my labor
but my limbs failed to produce
The danger of being cut down
remained constantly before me.
Then one day I walked into the Son
And the brightness of his glory
exposed your evil crime
So wicked and so vile
In leaving the shackles on the freedman's mind

A Little Straight

Colossians 2:8 "Beware lest any man spoil you through Philosophy and vain deceit after the tradition of men..."

In this world of crookedness,
Crooked love, crooked teachers,
Crooked faith, crooked preachers
I'm trying to give the world a little straight
Straight talk, straight truth, straight faced
We're loosing our children to a world
That is cruel hard and blurred
To rectify we must start with truth
No more Santa Clause
No more fairies for their tooth
Today is the day to change their fate
If we start with a little straight

Love
In a Name

Christ Jesus

John 14:2 "...I go to prepare a place for you."

Come go with me
High above the trees, where
Rivers flow eternally
Inside a space
So filled with grace
Thanksgiving and God's mercy
Just visualize first in your mind
Each blessing being answered
Soon you will see
Unveiled to thee
Something glorious and miraculous

Nicole

Luke 1:45 "...blessed is she that believed...."

Now I wanted the Lord
I wanted no other thing
Confused and alone, until
Omnipotence came
Love laid me to rest
Elevated my mind
Now I am awaken
The old me
Frozen in time
For I move throughout eternity
Peeking here and there
Reborn a new creature
To live forever and ever

Clarice

1 Corinthians 13:13 "...and the greatest of these is Love."

Close your eyes and visualize
Laying down with me
Above the sky, where
Rivers flow crystal clear, from
Inside an angel's wings we peer, while
Coming into the Promised Land
Entrance is granted and
We can see where we will spend eternity
And now Clarice, I hope you see
My love is for always, but
When always will cease to be
My love will never fade

Debbie

Matthew 14:14 "If ye shall ask any thing in my name,
I will do it."

Did you make your request known... in
Entirety to our Lord
Before his throne of grace
Brought from deep within your heart
It is no mystery to him
Each wish he already sees
But you must first speak them
To show that you believe

Demetria

Ephesians 5:28 "So ought men to love their wives as their own bodies."

Day after day
Each morning of my life
My heart beats strong for you
Each day I promise
To provide, because my love is true
Remember in the Garden of Eden
If I were
Adam and you were Eve
I never would have failed
To defend your honor night and day
And light would have prevailed

Gwen

Isaiah 62.11 "...Behold thy salvation cometh..."

God is with you
When it's hard to believe
Even at your
Notorious times
His eyes have always seen
Your sacrifice your test
They have not been in vain
For you shall reap a harvest
Of his blessed Latter Rain

Lakyra T. Garth

Hebrews 13:2 ""be not forgetful to entertain strangers for thereby some have entertained angels unawares."

Suffer the
Little children to come unto me
Angels I bring forth through thee
Kept hidden from the eyes of man
Your divine identity and plan, shall be
Revealed in God's on time
Awaken O daughter of Zion
Take thy place and lead the way
God has created
A new thing
Revelation shall come by woman
The children lead the way
Heaven's gates are open
By God's love, mercy, and grace

Mary

*Proverb 11:16 "A gracious woman
Retaineth honor..."*

My heart can feel your pain
Although my eyes can't see...and
Right before you spoke the words
Your Savior turned his face to thee
He saw his beautiful daughter
Stand up against the world
And he was very proud of
His precious baby girl
No prayer has gone unanswered
No wish has he declined
And now you will receive it all
Right before your eyes

Lady Doris

Proverbs 14:1 "Every wise woman buildeth her house..."

Lady wisdom you have a foundation
And now it is time to build
Do not delay any longer
Your harvest is ready to yield
Deposit your love with interest
Open up your heart
Receive the latter rain of blessing
Increase that will never part
Shine for your salvation has come

Mary

Proverbs 31:26 "She openeth her mouth with wisdom; And in her tongue is the law of kindness."

Mary, did you know
Angels are at your side...on your
Right and on your left
Your protection God provides
My mind never wondered
Why you walked in such glory
You spoke with such strong love
I knew that it was sent from
Heaven up above

Ora Lee

1 Corinthians 15:51 "Behold, I show you a mystery; we shall not all sleep, but we shall all be changed."

One day love will lift you
Right before our eyes
Away into God's heaven
Letting this world's pain subside
Eternal life with the Master
Earth is not your home
And deep within our hearts
Your presence we will long
But in the midnight hour
You'll visit in our dreams
And it can be so real if only we believe

Serita P. Lane

*Psalms 27:13 "I had fainted unless I believed to see
The goodness of the Lord in the Land of the living"*

*Shout Hallelujah
Everyday of your life, your
Reward is at hand
Into the Master's Rest you've
Taken comfort
Adhering to his every command
Peace unto you my sister
Let God's praises ring loud
A new beginning and
New life
Eternal he has allowed*

Shirley

Isaiah 62:12 "And they shall call them, the holy people, the redeemed of the Lord..."

Such a long journey
How much you've overcame
Instead of death you chose life
Relinquishing past pains
Live, ...for
Each day is new
Your yesterdays are just that
No one can longer hurt you
You are far past that
For you have overcame
The whole entire world...and
You're forever in God's rest,
His precious little girl

Vera

*Jeremiah 31:22 "...for the Lord hath created a new
Thing in the earth, a woman shall compass a man."*

*O what a glorious
Victory you have won...in each and
Every test you've glorified the Son
Restoration is here...just
Around the bend
New life, new beginning
To which there is no end
Fear not God's little soldier
He's right by your side
And there is where He'll always be
For the rest of your life*

Sister Shelton

Jeremiah 20:9 "...his word was in my heart
As a burning fire shut up in my bones..."

Shine forth your light
It is not intended to be hidden
So many all around you are in
Total darkness
Experience you have
Right from the hand of God
So why deny the sheep the food
Home grown from deep inside of you
Election you obtained over a year ago
Lord Jesus anointed you
To teach the truth in whole
Only you can bring forth this message
No one else has lived your life
So deliver it with power
God's ambassador of light

Sister Banks

Isaiah 62:10 "...lift up a standard for the people..."

Silently you waited while
Intently looking in
Slow to speak quickly to listen
Teaching the flock as your soul glistens
Express your gratitude, yet
Relay to the congregation the truth
Brought to you from
Above by God's angels
No more turning a deaf ear pretending not to see
Keep your hand in God's for through you he
Shall speak
To give them all a warning
That they must change their ways
The Savior has returned it is the final days

Sister Ryland

Jeremiah 1:17 "Say not I am a child for thou shalt go to all that I shall send thee and whatsoever I command thee thou shalt speak"

*So you say
Inside, who am I to teach
Such important message cannot be
Taught by me
Each day it is more obvious to discern
Right and wrong
Revelations come to you from God
You cannot hide them anymore…your
Love for God is stronger than the
Average man..
No request has he forsaken
Dorothy you are mistaken
For you have been elected into God's divine plan
And you shall bring forth God's word to his lost
children*

Shumeka and Eric

Mark 10:9 "...What therefore God hath joined
Together let no man put asunder..."

So I shall share my life with you
Holding on to these words of truth
Unconditional is our love
My soul rejoiced the day
Eternally you vowed to stay
Keeping me forever yours
Angels will clear our path
As we journey hand and hand
No weapon formed will dare trespass
Didn't God give you to me?...for
Ever after and eternity
Right here we both shall be
Inside the master's hand
Complete from beginning to end

Carina, Carina

Isaiah 9:6 "For unto us
a child is born..."

Can't wait to see this child
Adorned with rings of gold
Remember children are from God
Into your womb now bestowed
Now do not doubt your blessing
Always have faith and believe
Carina God has a gift for you
Arriving from your childhood dreams
Rico is included
I know you love him so
Now let his love take over
And the blessings overflow

Clarence

Matthew 5:36 "...Be not afraid, only believe."

Clap your hands and stomp your feet
Lift your hands up with praise
Arriving from our Master
Rewards Deliverance and Grace
Ending all hurt misery and pain
No weapon formed has prospered
Can you feel the Latter Rain?
Each drop you should saver
Each day will be brand new
And you shall receive it all from God
A life that is brand new

Rhonda

Mark 10:16 "And he took them up in his arms,
Put his hands upon them, and blessed them.

Righteousness is measured by your faith
Hope your faith is overflowing
One need not ask another
No one else bears your anointing
Don't doubt what he has for you
A wish a dream comes true,
A life that is brand knew
Is waiting just for you
Straight from the master's hand

Carolyn and Keith

"Song of Solomon 8:6 "...for Love is as strong as death..."

Can the wind blow?
And the earth not know
Remember this when
One of you is alone
Love my dears once planted
Yearly yields
No famine or drought only wide open fields
And love my darlings
Needs spirit to survive
Don't you know love is divine?
Keep trying to separate you'll only draw close
Each pull only strengthens the knot in the rope
It's divinely tied
Together by three
Hope Love Faith the Holy Trinity

Kelsie

Esther 2:17 "he set the royal crown upon her head,
And made her queen..."

Keep your eyes on the prize
Each and everyday
Life has dealt you a blow
So God shall show you the way
I know it seems so far away, but
Eventually you shall see
That God has blessed and exalted you
My child you are a queen

Shirley

Proverbs 3:24 ..." yea, thou shalt lie down,
And thy sleep shall be sweet."

So much struggle and toil
Has god forsaken me?
I know that he has not
Rain falls too plentifully
Lord thank you for your Grace
Each drop of your Mercy
Your loving arms are my pillow
The bed of which I sleep

Jermaine

*Isaiah 60:1 "Arise, shine for thy light is come
And the glory of the Lord is risen upon thee."*

*Just imagine what your life will be for you are
Eternally in the rest of God
Remove your covering of sin, for you young
Man have been born again
A rise shine like the king you are
Into the kingdom there is an open door
None one can
Ever close*

Billy White

Isaiah 60:1 "Arise shine for thy Light is come
And the Glory of the Lord is risen upon thee."

Because of your faithfulness'
It's your time
Life more abundant is your prize
Lift up his name
Your light will shine
Why second guess the spirit guides
Hard to believe, but
I can see
The present Glory
Each victory

Minnie

Proverbs 31:31 "Give her of the fruit of her hands; and let her own works praise her in the gates."

Many days add up to months and flow
Into years
Now a new life is beginning
Now there is life without fears
I pray you many blessing
Everyone only the best
Each day shall be new
Enjoy your hard earned rest

Tawanda

Song of Solomon 1:12
"My lover is to me a sachet of myrrh..."

Today is a special day
And you are a special lady
Wish you all the best of love
Allow no doubts or maybe's
Now that you are in my life
Days are so much brighter
And I count you as a blessing
To take me higher and higher

Sadie

Esther 1:11 "...for she was fair to look upon."

Such a beautiful lady
And still there's more to see
Don't know if you know it yet
I plan to cherish thee
Each day lets become friends
Just pass away the day
From here on out no strings
Just want to know your way
Christmas comes in December
With you it comes in May
Let me get to know you
Just want to know your way

Glennis

1 Corinthians 13:13 "...but the greatest of these is love."

Gifts from God are beautiful
Love is the greatest of these
Each year has been a gift of
New love growing into eternity
Nineteen years together
In all sorts of stormy weather
So Happy Anniversary lady
May our love last forever

Sabrina

Song of Solomon 1:15 "How Beautiful you are, my darling

*Sharing life with you has been wonderful
And our children are divine
Being your husband has been so joyful
Right know our life is more than fine
I see you as so beautiful
No other can compare
A life with you and Our Master
May we live for ever and ever*

Alexander

"The Great One"
Psalms 113:8 "That he may set him with princes, even with the princes of his people."

I look upon you
And see the greatness in man
Strong with heart conceived in iniquity
To be reborn in the spirit
The choicest of men
Able to lead one from sin
Into a life of greatness
I pray these blessings over you
Speak life into you
So that God may flow through you
For the good of me and you
Alexander "The great one"
Man of God, Man of truth

Bianca

Song of Solomon 2:13 "...Arise, my love,
my fair one, and come away."

Before I met you
I longed for you
A woman to share my dreams with
Now that you're here, let me with
Care, ask that you
Allow me your love to run away with

Bobby Jean Lenoir

John 20:22 "And when he had said this, he breathed on them, and saith unto them, Receive ye the Holy Ghost:"

Before you were God knew you
Once you arrived he
Blew on you,
Blessing you with his love
You are my gift from heaven
Joy sent from God above
Each year
An angel prays increasing your days
Not a one will go unpaid, Jesus'
Love has paved the way
Eternity is yours
Now before you is the door
Overflowing
In heaven and in earth, your
Rewards have given birth

Canary

Matthew 12:42 *"The queen of the South shall rise up in judgment with this generation..."*

Can you be this lady
A queen to save the world
Now in preparation
Awaiting God's return
Rarest of beauties
You appear to me to be
I guess time will tell and
I will wait and see

Claudia

Mark 10:15 "...whosoever shall not receive the kingdom of God as a little child he shall not enter therein."

Can you stay this way forever
Like a little child
Always being kind
Untainted by adult life
Dolls and braids
Innocent and trained
An angel for always

George and Leshonda

Isaiah 62:12 "and they shall call them,
the holy people, the redeemed of the LORD..."

God gives us glimpses of paradise
Each morning in a beautiful sunrise
One day we will see the entire thing
Royal robes of blue and gold
Great valleys of milk and honey comb
Eternity with our king
And I pray to share it with you
Now, this
Day and forever more
Love will fill our cup
Erupting, overflowing
Spreading from one to the next
How I long for that day
One body one mind
No worries, no tears
Day after day after day
After day

Lakeisha

John 9:35 "...Dost thou believe on the Son of God?"

Like petals on the wind
Let his love fall down on you
Awaken to his will
Keep your choices true
Each day you will grow
Into a blessed seed
So give your greatest wish to God
He will answer
And heed

Pearl

Proverbs 31:10 "...for her price is far above rubies."

Place a crown upon your head
Elevate your mind and soul
An angel of God you are
Right here on Earth to behold
Light fills your being
So let your divineness shine
Always and forever
Until the end of time.

Ronell and Pearl

Psalm 28:8 "The Lord is their strength,
and he is the saving strength of his anointed."

Remember the beginning everything was new
One was not without the other being one
Not two
Each day brings new mercies
Love comes from high above
Life will have new meaning
As you grow in this new love
No weapon formed will prosper
Days will seem new again
Peace joy and happiness
Eternal life that has no end
And this grace he has showered upon you
Remember when you pray
Let him know you are grateful
each and every day

Sennie D House

*Matthew 19:26 "...But with God all
things are possible."*

*Set your sight on things above
Erase the thing below
Now God has many gifts for you
New blessings to bestow
I recommend to you Christ Jesus
Everlasting is his love
Don't hesitate to make a wish
Hope showers them from above
Only a God like ours
Understands our direst needs
So ask and you shall be given
Eternal love, God's righteous seed*

Shirleta Walker

*Isaiah 58:8 "...the glory of the LORD
shall be thy reward."*

*Surely you are blessed
Highly favored in the Lord
It is no mystery you see
Rich rewards are coming forth
Life has dealt you many blows, but
Eternal life will now be bestowed
Take and drink to your fill
As old wounds our God will heal
Walk upright in your faith
Always remember his divine grace
Let God's love overflow
Keep going always hold on
Everlasting blessing I speak over you
Rich rewards of love honor and truth*

Tasha

Psalm 23:5 "Thou prepares a table before me
in the presence of mine enemies;"

The Lord has prepared a blessing
A table extravagantly spread
Such royal blessings
Have you gained by obedience
A prayer has been answered
From deep within your soul
You are a royal princess
A glory to behold

Timon Edwards

Mark 10:14 "Suffer the little children to come unto me, ...for of such is the Kingdom of God."

Touch not my anointed
I dwell within their souls,
My vessel my servant
One my spirit over flows
No weapon formed can hurt you
Each
Day I will make new
With my hands I will shield every
Arrow from you
Rich blessings I send forth
Daily walk with me my son
Surely you are a blessing
A victory overcome

Vanessa

Proverbs 17:17 "A friend loveth at all times..."

Very few women can be called friend
An even lesser number if they are true
Now time has proven you well
Experience has guided us through
So I pray you accept this gift
So thought out to surprise
A wonderful friend you have shown
Yourself to be,
Glad to have you in my life

A~Keiya

Psalm 92:1 "It is a good thing to give thanks unto the LORD, and to sing praises unto thy name, O most High:"

Awesome is our God
Keeps you safe in his arms
Each day you'll give him praise
Into his rest go from harm
You know how to praise him
And praise him you will
You have a heavenly voice
And with his Spirit you are filled

Betty

Psalms 143:1 "Hear my prayer, O Lord, give ear to my supplications: in thy faithfulness answer me, and in thy righteousness.

Better days ahead of you
Each day I speak anew
Take one step at a time
To reveal God's divine
Year of blessing overflowing
The very things you have been wanting

Branden

Psalm 86:11 "Teach me thy way, O LORD;
I will walk in thy truth:

Before you knew your mother
Remember you knew the lord
And he is going to teach you
Now while you're a little boy
Don't hesitate to pray
Each day will bring new gifts
Now God hand is on you
And up to heaven he will lift

Briaunna

Psalm 81:1 "SING aloud unto God our strength:"

Before time began you sang
Right before the Lord
In his glorious kingdom
As angels looked
Upon
Now you will sing again
No one will know your song
Angels will teach you
Starting Easter Morn

Chanston J. Ford

Proverbs 3:1 "my son, forget not my law;
but let thine heart keep my commandments:

Children are an
Heritage of the Lord
A gift from heaven sent
No greater gift to receive
So special and so blessed
Today was a great day for you
One greater than your birth
New life has been given
Joy to the world again
Forever keep God close to you
One day you'll understand
Rewards heaven will send to you
Day after day without end

Derrick Shaw

Psalms 40:2 "He brought me up also out of an horrible pit, out of the miry clay, and set my feet upon a rock, and established my goings."

Didn't Our Father create
Earth and Heaven out of Chaos
Ripped through space to create time
Raised the dead and turned water
Into Wine
Can this same force be in you
Keeping you, recreating you
So a thing of beauty might arise, to
House God's Spirit so divine
Awake Son of God open your eyes
Welcome your new life above the skies

Ethan

Psalm 37:4 "Delight thyself also in the LORD; and he shall give thee the desires of thine heart."

Each day will be blessed for you
Today and forever more
Heaven is your home
And angels guard your door
No weapon formed can prosper
You life is so divine
You will live eternally
Beyond the end of time

Isaiah

Psalm 106:31 *"And that was counted unto him for righteousness unto all generations forevermore."*

I know Jesus loves you
Sent you from heaven's grace
And you will do great things
I know this is your fate
And you will save many
Help them find the Lord
You will be counted righteous
And become a son of God

Jaila

Psalm 34:1 "I will bless the LORD at all times:
his praise shall continually be in my mouth."

Jesus gave you a voice
An angelic song to sing
It is to him you will give praise
Lift your voice up to the King
A reward is waiting
God's work has begun
So give the Lord his due
On this Blessed Easter Morn

Jasmine

Matthews 27:63 "...After three days I will rise again."

Jesus rose on Easter Morning
And saved all the world
So Jasmine you are so special
Most importantly God's darling girl
I pray for you rich blessings
No wish to go unfilled
Each day you'll learn new lessons
And with wisdom be filled

Jeannetta

Romans 13:8 "Let no debt remain outstanding, except the continuing debt to love one another, for he who loves his fellowman has fulfilled the law."

Jesus gave us strict orders
Each one should love the other
And you have shown such love to me
Not unlike a spiritual mother
New beginnings are ahead of me
Each one begins with you
Today you open up a door
To allow Gods floodwaters through
And I am forever grateful
May God Bless and Honor you

Ny

Matthew 5:5 "Blessed are the meek:
for they shall inherit the earth.

No one knows what you shall be
Yet it will be reveal
The meek shall inherit the earth
And the thirsty shall be filled
Blessed are you Ny
For meekness is your seed
And it shall bear fruit,
For you will always believe

Ruquayah

Psalm 119:73 "Thy hands have made me and fashioned me:"

Remember your creator in the days of your youth
Understand his love and law
Question all that is untruth
Until the end of time
Angels guide your way
You are his perfect model
And you will
Hold truth on display

Sheila

Luke 12:32 "fear not little flock, for it is your
Father's good pleasure to give you the Kingdom."

She rises in the morning with love
Heaven has opened merciful doors
Each day will reveal a dream
It will reveal your destiny
Life eternal and divine peace
Always to you my queen

Sharon

Song of Solomon 1:2
"...for thy love is better than wine."

See you complete me
Hold me together piece by piece
Always by my side, I am
Reborn with you my wife
Over and over my world revives
Now just stay in my life and
I will never compromise, because
Your love to me is better than wine

Tiffney

Psalms 118:24 "This is the day which the LORD hath made; We will rejoice and be glad in it."

Today is the day the Lord declared
It, to bless the earth with you
For me it is as blessed, as my love is true
Forever beyond the end of time
No limits to God's plan divine
Everyday we will start anew
Your every wish and dream come true

Trey

Psalm 119:41 "Let thy mercies come also unto me, O LORD..."

Today is Easter Morning
Rise and praise the Lord
Even though you are young
You are a child whom HE adores

Aillean

*Psalms 23:2 "...He maketh me to lay
down in green pastures."*

*Awaiting you is a gift
Impossible to believe
Love flows from you
Like wind through the trees
Each path has been straight
Arriving at heaven's gate
Now walk in your blessing
And always share your faith*

Alisha

Esther 2:17 "he set the royal crown upon her head,
And made her queen..."

Allow the Father to make you
Life eternal you have gained
Into your life he is bringing a
Shower of blessings and gains
How wonderfully blessed you are
An angel in disguise
But your beauty shall be reveal
in God's blessed time

Andrea

*"Song of Solomon 8:6 "...for Love is
As strong as death..."*

Always a step ahead of me
Now you keep me in line
Don't every second guess
Real love is hard to find
Each day we get better
Always renewing our mind
Now we will stay together
Until the end of time

Jeanette

Luke 12:32 "fear not little flock, for it is your Father's good pleasure to give you the Kingdom."

Joy comes from God
Emptied into your soul
Arise for you have been reborn
Now you are strong and bold
Enter into the Kingdom
Take hold of everything
Today is a new day
Ever blessed by Jesus our King

Mary Jean

*Proverbs 31:10 "...for her price
Is far above rubies..."*

*Mom you are my strength
Always uplifting me
Remember the hard times
Yes, now life has become easy
Just stay as you are
Each day is brand new
And God has a miracle
Now unfolding for you*

Mike and Lisette

Ephesians 5:25 "Husbands love your wives..."

My father loves me
I accept his will, and through his
Kindness a divine plan has been revealed
Eternal life
And eternal love
Now the two are blessed from above
Daily we shall be reborn
Like the wind rides the wing of doves
I have been raised into the arms of
Such love and
Each day I will renew my strength
To you, for you
To be the best man
Ever to cross your path
Because with you my soul is blessed

www.ingramcontent.com/pod-product-compliance
Lightning Source LLC
Chambersburg PA
CBHW070833100426
42813CB00003B/602